CRICUT FOR BEGINNERS

The Complete Step – by – Step Guide for your Cricut Design Space with Illustrations. Tips and Tricks Easy to Apply Even if you are a Beginner

Megan Jones

Copyright – 2021 - All rights reserved. The content contained within this book may not be reproduced, duplicated or transmitted without direct written permission from the author or the publisher. Under no circumstances will any blame or legal responsibility be held against the publisher, or author, for any damages, reparation, or monetary loss due to the information contained within this book. Either directly or indirectly. Legal Notice: This book is copyright protected. This book is only for personal use. You cannot amend, distribute, sell, use, quote or paraphrase any part, or the content within this book, without the consent of the author or publisher. Disclaimer Notice: Please note the information contained within this document is for educational and entertainment purposes only. All effort has been executed to present accurate, up to date, and reliable, complete information. No warranties of any kind are declared or implied. Readers acknowledge that the author is not engaging in the rendering of legal, financial, medical or professional advice. The content within this book has been derived from various sources. Please consult a licensed professional before attempting any techniques outlined in this book. By reading this document, the reader agrees that under no circumstances is the author responsible for any losses, direct or indirect, which are incurred as a result of the use of information contained within this document, including, but not limited to, - errors, omissions, or inaccuracies

Table of contents

INTRODUCTION
CHAPTER 1: What is Cricut Machine and what It does?
CHAPTER 2: Setting up the cricut machine
CHAPTER 3: Everything about design space
CHAPTER 4: What is cricut access?
CHAPTER 5: Cricut access FAQ
CHAPTER 6: Getting started on your first project
CONCLUSION

INTRODUCTION

You're assuredly looking for a simple guide to start up with this beautifully inventive machine whether you've recently purchased or are dreaming of buying a Cricut machine. Therefore, this guide has been designed for your festivities and learning. The Cricut machine in a revolutionary system with diverse implementations through a range of project designs.

Its main purpose is to create professional quality cuts in practically every kind of material. This helps you to literally build everything you can envision. Besides that, you're not going to have to waste a lot of time cutting patterns. This machine takes all the conjecture from generating forms and photographs that give life to the most creative ideas. However, you may not be completely aware of the way the Cricut machine operates. This book is designed to provide you with the basics you need to use the machine as a real professional. And besides, there is no reason to fail to try to work out this revolutionary system.

What you need to begin with is simply and concisely described in this book. On the subsequent sections, you will find out what you need to go forward with the development of creative designs by using Cricut machine. Every chapter has been intended to help you get the best out of your Cricut machine. This is particularly true if you're thinking of doing it as part of a business plan. In this respect, the use of this apparel magic machine is critical to you immediately. We're going to look at how you can use the Cricut machine to make several of the most innovative and artistic creations you can conceive of. Most of all, you're not going to have to breach the bank to make innovative ideas that would definitely impress your friends and family. In comparison, you won't have to waste long hours studying how to master the computer and the program. It's all built to help you get off the ground fast. Quite significantly, this guide is simple to use and to pursue.

In this way, the installation of your Cricut machine and the program "Design Space" will begin easily. Most significantly, we're going to guide you by the most essential points to remember before you get started on your very first project. This provides a strong description of how Production Space works, and also the import of images which you can use to make your designs come alive. With that in view, creativity is the only requirement for the Cricut unit. Work to get the best out of your thoughts by placing them into effect. There's no reason to hang back. You already have all of the designs and prototypes you need to create. This helps you to create more complicated designs gradually.

Eventually, you'll make professional creations that will definitely inspire those around you. Thank you very much for considering this book. There are other alternatives out there for you to select on this topic. By selecting this book, you're taking a step in the right direction. It's also rewarding to realize that you understand the hard work that has gone into making this guide. You're bound to be excited to get started with your Cricut machine. So, without any further delay, we're going to get down to work.

CHAPTER 1 - What is Cricut Machine and what It does?

Cricut machines are getting tremendous prominence in the crafting community, since they no longer have cartridges like older machines, and now it is handled digitally. This helps you to use shapes and fonts as long as you want it to be on your computer. Machines have specialized features to work with Wi-Fi or Bluetooth. You can build your iPhone, device or iPad from this.

One of the great thing about such machines is that there are several projects that you can try to use materials.One of the great thing about such machines is that there are several projects that you can try to use materials. It is said the Cricut machine is a die-cutting machine. They are often related to printers in several respects. A printer can print the template you created on your screen. A Cricut, though, can cut the pattern out of any material you want to use.

You should use it as a printer. If you plan to do this, there's an adapter slot on your desktop, and then you need to load a marker on it. Then you'll make the computer sketch the template for you, and it'll give your designs a lovely hand-written look. Each machine has unique ways to cut items, and you'll be able to experience it, based on which machine you have. You can cut different materials for different designs, as well as leather bracelets. These machines are designed for extremely detailed cuts and can cut about a hundred various materials. The maker, the fourth machine we are about to address, can cut everything else, and over 100 other materials, particularly fabrics. The Cricut machine also arrives with its own software, which makes it easier to render your creations, and helps you to upload photos too. The software allows you to buy, build, or upload photos, and enables you to import cuts also.

The earlier machines used cartridges, we described above. If the latest cartridges are not, you should be able to use them on your new computer because you have an older cartridge. You will find that the files you need for your needs and purposes are absolutely intact. You do not need a cartridge because now that it is finished online, you have access to a large library of cuts and files and this machine can even be etched. Gravure is a hot product right now, and because of that, all of those computers hop to get one so they can do this. Even so, you should remember before buying a computer like this. There are several alerts. They are available in the biggest locations, so that you have no problems.

It is not advised that you purchase this machine everywhere except explicitly from the website itself and not from a third party; some of the most popular internet stores are not the safest way to buy this machine. If you're headed to a shop like Hobby Lobby or Joann, they're healthy shops because they've been verified to give you exactly what you're buying, but there's also a decline in shopping from these outlets.

In the supermarket, costs are higher of what you'll find on the machine's own website, and you can't use discounts for any of the Cricut items that the store is selling. In comparison, you're not expecting to be allowed to find a kit deal; they're being put together on the Cricut platform primarily to save you a bunch of money and give you the chance to buy extra tools you're likely to need for a decent price.

Another famous retailer is Amazon, and, as we said earlier, online third-party sellers are not good choices to purchase from them. Most craftsmen prefer to purchase their cutting machines, especially from the website, because there have been problems with Amazon. That's extremely risky to make larger transactions from sites like Amazon, because while you're covered by their refund policies, it doesn't stop you from dealing with shipments that have gone wrong or lost pieces. Even the key pieces were incomplete in some cases. Amazon costs are certainly cheaper, but they are generally only a few bucks apart, so it doesn't feel worth it.

What Can I Do with A Cricut Machine?

There are plenty of activities you can do with the Cricut machine! There is no way that I can even mention all the solutions, but here are some common projects that provide you with an idea of what the machine can do.

- Cut out funny forms and characters for scrapbooking
- Make personalized, crafted cards for every special occasion (here is an example)
- Fashion a one or a t-shirt (here's an example)
- Make a bracelet of leather
- Render buntings and other party decorations;
- Make your own painting stencils (here is an example)
- Make a vinyl sticker for the car window

- Tag items in your storeroom, or in a playroom

- Make your monogram pillows

- Build your own Christmas ornaments (here is an example)

- Addressing the packet

- Adorn the mug, cup, or tumbler (here is an example)

- Etch glass at home (here is an example)

- Make your own decals on the wall

- Create a sign of painted wood

- Create clings to your own window

- Cut appliances or quilt squares

- Build a stand mixer for decals

The Different Cricut Models

Cricut Explore One
The Explore One is a wired die cutting machine that can cut a wide range of materials from paper to cloth and more. This machine has 1 tool slot relative to all other versions actually sponsored that have two. Note: there is a Bluetooth wireless adapter available to buy individually.

Cricut Explore Air

Explore Air is a wireless die cutting system that can cut a wide range of materials from paper to bonded cloth. This unit is basically much like its second version, in addition to housing and slower cutting capability. This model has two spaces, one for the pens and the other for the knives.

Cricut Explore Air 2

The Explore Air 2 is a slight overhaul of the Explore Air line, which has introduced three colors (Mint Blue, Rose Anna, Giffin Lilac). Also it introduced Quick Mode to cut vinyl, iron-on heat transfer vinyl, and card stock at up to 2x speeds.

Cricut Maker

The Cricut Maker is a new model, launched on August 20, 2017, intended to cut thicker materials like balsa wood, basswood, non-bonded cloth, leather and felt.[4] The Maker is the first Cricut system that facilitates the use of a Rotary Blade for the straight cutting of fabric and a single or double score wheel with different pressure to score thicker paper than that of the original scoring stylus that uses a Rotary Blade for the straight cutting of fabric. In mid-2019, Cricut launched four more tips for use in QuickSwap homes. Standing tip, embossing tip, wavy blade and perforation blade.

Cricut Accessories & Supplies Every Beginner Needs

For cricut projects, the following accessories are essential to work well

- Cricut blades
- Cricut mats: spiegare

- Scoringo tools

- Additional tools

- Tool kit

- Bluethoot adapter

- **Cricut blades**: It can be ambiguous to identify which Cricut blades you need and the materials that they cut from there. But learning how to adjust your blades and pick the one that is ideally suited to your project is an invaluable lesson to learn as a rookie. Multiple blades do different stuff and operate with different equipment, both of which sound pretty daunting as a novice, but don't worry, because I'm going to clarify all below.

WHICH BLADES WORK WITH YOUR CRICUT?

Not all of the Cricut blades are synchronized with all machines. This map is a perfect reference guide to know which blades are operating on your machine.

WHICH BLADE DO I NEED FOR MY PROJECT?

The blade you use is classified by the characteristics of material you cut. The blade insights below will help you identify which blades have what purpose.

Premium Fine-Point Blade

The blade is manufactured to make the most precise cuts and it is the most versatile blade. This can be marked with its gold housing (older blades may be silver). The Cricut Premium Fine-Point Blade arrives with all new Cricut Builder and Cricut Explore family machines.

What Does the Premium Fine-Point Blade Cut?

- Paper
- Cardstock
- Vinyl
- Iron-On Vinyl
- Washi Tape
- Parchment Paper
- And other medium weight materials

Deep Point Blade

This blade is identical to the Precision Fine-Point Blade, but has a steeper blade angle. The Deep Point Blade is capable of cutting tougher substances. Its black housing may be recognized. It is congruent with the Cricut Maker and Cricut Explore family.

What Does the Deep Point Blade Cut?

- Cardboard
- Chipboard
- Corrugated Paper
- Foam Sheets
- Leather
- Magnetic Sheets
- Some Fabrics
- Stiffened Felt
- Thick Cardstock

- And other thicker materials

Bonded-Fabric Blade

The Bonded-Fabric Blade gives you all of the characteristics of the Premium Fine-Point Blade. This can be described by a pink case matching the pink color of the Cricut FabricGrip mat. It is congruent with the Cricut Maker and Cricut Explore family.

Note: This blade is used only with fabrics bound to the backing stock.

What does the Bonded-Fabric Blade cut?

- Bonded Fabrics
- Fabrics With An Iron-On Backer

Rotary Blade

The Rotary Blade slices into nearly every fabric with no need for a backrest material. It also fits well with fragile materials such as toilet paper and liquor. It can be used with a pink FabricGrip mattress. The Rotary Blade is arriving in the drive housing. It's just congruent with the Cricut Maker.

What does the Rotary Blade cut?

- Bonded Fabric
- Burlap
- Canvas
- Cashmere
- Chiffon
- Cotton Fabric
- Denim
- Duck Cloth

- Faux Leather
- Faux Suede
- Felt
- Flannel
- Fleece
- Jersey
- Jute
- Knits
- Leather
- Linen
- Metallic Leather
- Moleskin
- Muslin
- Oil Cloth
- Polyester
- Printable Fabric
- Seersucker
- Silk
- Terry Cloth

- Tulle
- Tweed
- Velvet
- Wool Felt

Knife Blade

This blade cuts into dense materials up to 3/32" thick. It fits well with modest detail cuts. Using this blade to cut the purple StrongGrip mat. The Knife Blade is arriving in the drive housing. It's just congruent with the Cricut Maker.

What does the Knife Blade cut?

- Balsa
- Basswood
- Craft Foam
- Heavy Chipboard

- Matboard

- Leather

Scoring Wheel

The scoring wheel does what it seems like—creating crisp creases in thick and thin fabrics to make accurate folds. Functionally, it's not a sword, but it makes detailed score lines rather than complete cuts. It's just consistent with the Cricut Maker.

The Score Wheel comes in QuickSwap Casing, which implies that adjusting the tip is as easy as pressing a button. This is helpful because Cricut makes both single and double score wheels so it's good to be able to swap them using the same housing.

The Score Wheel makes one deep score line, whereas the Double Score Wheel produces two parallel score lines (useful on heavier materials).

What materials does the Single Scoring Wheel score?

- Acetate
- Cardstock
- Construction Paper
- Copper
- Copy Paper
- Corrugated Paper
- Crepe Paper
- Embossed Foil Paper
- Flocked Paper
- Foil Acetate
- Foil Posterboard

- Glitter Cardstock
- Grocery Bag
- Handmade Paper
- Holographic Cardstock
- Kraft Cardstock
- Origami
- Parchment Paper
- Pearl Paper
- Photo Paper
- Plastic Canvas
- Sticky Note
- Tattoo Paper
- Vellum
- Wax Paper
- Wrapping Paper

What materials does the Double Scoring Wheel score?

- Cardboard
- Cereal Box
- Cork

- Corrugated Cardstock
- Craft Foam
- Foil Paper
- Poster Board
- Heavy Cardstock
- Heavy Paper
- Kraft Board
- Light Chipboard
- Shimmer Paper
- Sparkle Paper
- Watercolor Paper

Debossing Tip

The Debossing Tip is built to add nuance and artistic prowess to paper and leather designs. It depresses the template into the material effortlessly and you can instantly turn to another blade because it uses QuickSwap Housing! The Debossing Tip is compliant with the Cricut Maker only.

Use the Debossing Tip on the following materials:

- Adhesive Sheet, Double-Sided
- Cardstock
- Chipboard
- Construction Paper
- Copy Paper
- Craft Foam
- Deluxe Paper
- Duct Tape Sheet
- Faux Leather
- Flocked Paper
- Foil Acetate
- Foil Holographic Kraft Board
- Foil Poster Board

- Freezer Paper
- Genuine Leather
- Glitter Paper
- Heavy Watercolor Paper
- Kraft Board
- Matboard
- Poster Board
- Sticker Paper – Removable
- Sicky Note
- Tooling Leather
- Transparency
- Velum

Engraving Tip

The Engraving Tip is ideal for monograming or applying text and designs to a range of materials. It can write long sentences or plain shapes and logos, and can only be used with the Cricut Creator and the QuickSwap Housing. I assume that this would be a nice customized present to add a monogram to a leather tag for cosmetic bags!

The Engraving Tip works with:

- Acrylic
- Anodized aluminum
- Flat, soft metals
- Leather
- Plastic

Perforation Blade

There are too many options with the Perforation Blade, from tickets with stubs to coupon books to quotation books with interchangeable pages. Use this blade to create tearable projects, such as straight and curved tears. This blade is working with Cricut Creator and QuickSwap Housing. You will use the perforation blade below:

- Acetate
- Cardstock
- Foam
- Foil
- Paper
- Some Fabrics

Wavy Blade

This blade easily brings beautifully detailed edges to every style. Use it to create polished edges that make you feel fancy and look beautiful. The Wavy Blade fits well for the following:

- Cardstock
- Iron-On
- Paper
- Some Fabrics
- Vinyl

What can the Cricut Joy blade cut?

- Cardstock
- Corrugated Cardboard
- Faux Leather
- Flat Cardboard
- Foil Acetate
- Foil Poster Board
- Glitter Cardstock
- Iron-On Materials
- Paper
- Party Foil
- Vinyl
- Window Cling

The "Cricut Mat" is the surface where you cut all your designs. Right now, there are four different styles of mattresses, Soft Grip (blue), Standard Grip (green), Strong Grip (purple) and Fabric Grip (pink). Based on the product you're dealing with, you'll need a specific mat.

Cricut Machine Mat Tips

The Blue LightGrip Machine Mat has just the right grip to keep the material securely in place while cutting, yet enables rapid removal of the lighter weight material when you're done cutting. The LightGrip System Mat is best suited for lightweight fabrics, particularly:
- Printer paper
- Vellum
- Light cardstock paper
- Thin scrapbook paper
- <u>Washi sheets</u>
- Wrapping paper
- Construction paper

StandardGrip – Green Mat

The StandardGrip mat is the most popular and inexpensive mat built to work with medium-weight materials.

It normally comes with the buying of every Cricut Machine (make sure to read the description of the product admittedly), and it's green.

The most popular materials that can be cut with StandardGrip or Green Mat are:

- Cardstock
- HTV (Heat Transfer Vinyl)

- Permanent or removable vinyl

The purple StrongGrip Machine Pad provides a high hold surface ideal for heavy-duty materials. This mat is ideal for heavy-duty fabrics, along with:
- Thick cardstock
- Glitter cardstock
- Magnet material
- Chipboard
- Poster board
- Mat board
- Fabric with stiffener
- Corrugated cardboard
- (Faux) leather and suede
- Wood

Use the StrongGrip Machine Mat to create easy-to-use photo magnets with printable magnet sheets.

If you're an enthusiastic builder who wants to play with a multitude of products, the Strong-Grip mat complements the Cricut Maker knife blade. It's a must-have combination for cutting through heavy materials such as wood, mat, chipboard, and handcrafted foam. Build your own mat picture frame using the StrongGrip mat and knife blade pair, then add contoured accents with the braiding tip.

FabricGrip – Pink Mat

The FabricGrip mat is specially designed for the cutting of cloth. Linked with some of the Cricut family machines, or only on its own with the Rotary blade and the Cricut Maker.

The most popular materials that can be cut with the Firm Grip Mat are:

- Bonded fabric (Explore family machine)
- Any type of fabric with the rotary blade and Cricut Maker

ABOUT THE CRICUT TOOLS

There are actually two separate instruments for Cricut scoring: the Score Type and the Score Wheel. The Scoring Stylus can be used in the accessory clamp of any Cricut Explore or Cricut Maker unit. The Score Wheel, on the other hand, can only be found in a Cricut Builder. Both the stylus and the wheel perform high, but the wheel will apply more pressure and get a deeper, better score. Using everything you've got.

1. WEEDER

This method really is a must-have when it comes to Cricut crafting! If you're not yet comfortable with weeding, you'll be here soon. Technically, as your Cricut cuts fabrics like vinyl or iron-on, you'll need to remove the extra content outside your design and within your design. Generally, you're deleting the negative space so you can get to the plan. You're going to need a weeder in your life.

2. SCRAPER

The scraper is another must-have tool, so you can need it almost every time you use the Cricut! In your Cricut art, you can use your scraper in a variety of different ways. Next, it helps to adhere the materials to the mat before you slit it. Until you cut the stuff, you want to make sure that the material is completely smooth on the floor—the scraper can help remove any residue that you might have trapped on the surface, as well as any air bubbles. The scraper tool may also be used to separate materials from the mattress and to add vinyl/transfer tape to surfaces.

3. BASIC TOOL SET

This five-piece tool kit is one of our most famous tool sets. It comes with five blades, two of which we've already written about: a weeder, a scraper, and a scissor, a tweezer, and a spatula. This is a perfect tool kit to get if you're just heading out in the world of Cricut.

Next up, the scissors. I think it's pretty clear how you're going to use these in your Cricut craft.

First, tweezers can be useful for adding minor information to your designs, weeding vinyl/iron-on or scraping hot carrier sheets.

Last but not least, the spatula is already included in this box. This is yet another simple tool—it can help you extract materials from your mat.

4. BRAYER

Brayer was initially developed to help the Cricut Maker add fabric to cutting mats.

5. SCORING STYLUS

Scoring stylus is a best tool to have on hand if you want to create paper crafts! Your Cricut will keep the score stylus to build folding lines for you. Now you can conveniently make stamps, envelopes, 3D project boxes and more! The score stylus works on both the Cricut Explore Air 2 and the Cricut Maker.

6. PAPER TOOL SET

Since we're discussing about paper design, if you do a lot of paper crafts, like 3D flowers, you may want to look into getting this paper tool package. It comes with four tools: a precision piercer, a quilling tool, an easy edge grinder and a self-healing pad. I might suggest that if you were particularly into paper crafting, this would be a must-have product in your craft room!

7. PORTABLE TRIMMER

You should take out just what you need and cut it in straight lines. And you can quickly calculate what you need to cut the trimmer, so you can make the same cuts! There is indeed a swing-out arm that helps you to straighten your supplies, weigh, and then cut just what you need.

If you're new to the world of Cricut crafting, I strongly recommend the trimmer. I also strongly advise buying this Cricut Essential Tool Kit.

It comes with the trimmer, all the items in the simple tool kit that we spoke about earlier {scissors, scraper, spatula, tweezers, weeder}, and it even comes with a score stylus. It's really the best value for your buck, plus you're going to get a bunch of tools with it.

.

8. SEWING KIT

This recommendation is for the Cricut Maker only.

As you already know, the Cricut Maker is capable of cutting through the fabric. It's a truly amazing technology! If you're already an ardent sewer, you might have a lot of these things in your hand.

It comes with seven pieces: the pin cushion, the cloth shears, the seam ripper, the thread snaps, the buttons, the measuring tape and the leather thimble. All the necessary sewing and crafting things with your Cricut!

9. SELF-HEALING ROTARY MAT

You might just want to grab a double-sided self-healing mat when we're dreaming about sewing! This is a rotary cutting mat, but I really enjoy using my mat to do more than just cut the fabric on. I want to do much of my crafting on top of that, so I don't waste or destroy my desk. They are 18x24" and come in two distinct colors: mint and rose. One side has a good pattern while the other has a grid with 30, 45 and 60 degree markings.

10. TRUE CONTROL KNIFE

The TrueControl Knife is last, but not least. This is essentially a Xacto knife, so it's easier to WAY! Because of how it was made, you will get more control over your tasks by using the TrueControl Knife vs. the Xacto knife. A wide range of materials can be cut, such as paper, cardboard, thin plastics, cloth, cloth and more. It has a rubber handle that helps you to get a strong grip and comes with five interchangeable blades that you can quickly change without having to touch the blade. It's a small, but powerful tool!

BLUETOOTH ADAPTER

Both the Cricut Explore Air 2 and the Cricut Builder machines are Bluetooth compliant. You just need to connect your machine with your device to use Bluetooth with your machine.

You can use both Mac and Windows computers and also Android and iOS users. Both machines use Cricut DesignSpace to build the templates that your device will use.

Carefully cut some in-box wrapping, the cricot machine can be conveniently gripped by a cricket pen, the high-end blade housing and a welcome pack of resource supplies, power and USB cable housing the cricust manufacturer.

Start by injecting the power cable into the circular hole at the back of the unit.

Setting up our crypto builder on a USB computer

Safe the square-shaped end of the USB CABLE INTO of the available port on the back of the manufacturer.

Then insert the USB end on your laptop or desktop device.

Open a web browser and type the design of cricut.com for flash setup in the search bar.

Build a cricut ID by filling in the appropriate fields on the form.

Download the plug-in and read the instructions on the computer to mount the softwer.

Open the machine by raising the top cap, then control the machine.

When signed into the design field, follow the on-screen instructions to take a tour and start designing.

CHAPTER 2 – SETTING UP THE CRICUT MACHINE

How do I pair my Cricut Explore or Cricut Maker machine via Bluetooth?

You can cut wirelessly using Cricut Maker and Cricut Explore machines via Bluetooth. Follow the steps below to pair them with your computer or mobile device:

Note: Cricut Explore and Cricut Explore One require a Wireless Bluetooth Adapter to cut wirelessly.

 -Windows

 - Mac

 -iOS

 - Android

Setting up a Cricut Machine on Windows

1-Ensure that your Cricut Explore or Cricut Maker machine is turned on and within 10-15 feet of your desktop. Whether you have a Cricut Explore or a Cricut Explore One, make sure that your Bluetooth Wireless Adapter is inserted.

2-Most computers have Bluetooth enabled. Contrary, to decide if your computer is Bluetooth enabled, right-click the Start button and choose device Manager

3-If Bluetooth is mentioned, Bluetooth is activated on your device. If this is not the case, you would need to buy a USB gadget called a Bluetooth Dongle to allow your machine to connect to other Bluetooth devices.

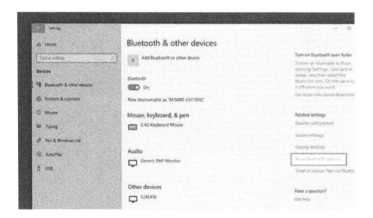

4- Close Device Manager.

5- Open the Start menu and select Settings.

6. Open the Devices option

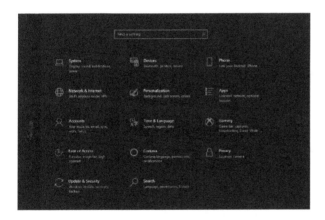

7. Ensure that Bluetooth is ON and click Add Bluetooth or other device.

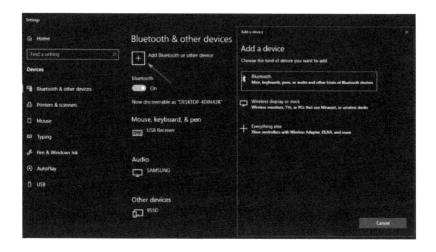

8. Select Bluetooth and wait for the computer to detect your Cricut machine. Select your machine from the list

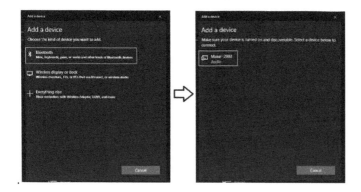

9. If you're prompted to enter a PIN, type 0000. Then select Connect

10. Your Cricut Maker or Cricut Explore is now paired with your Windows computer!

Setting up a Cricut Machine on Mac

1. Ensure that your Cricut Explore or Cricut Maker unit is turned on and within 10-15 feet of your computer. Whether you have a Cricut Explore or a Cricut Explore One, make sure that your Bluetooth Wireless Adapter is connected.

2. Most of the computers are Bluetooth® enabled. Though, to decide if your Mac is Bluetooth enabled, open Apple Menu > System Preferences and check for the Bluetooth® option.

3. Open the Bluetooth® screen. If Bluetooth is off, click the button to turn it on. Pick the name of your adapter/Bluetooth module from the list.

4. Ensure that your Cricut Explore or Cricut Maker machine is turned on and within 10-15 feet of your mobile device. Whether you have a Cricut Explore or a Cricut Explore One, make sure that your Bluetooth Wireless Adapter is connected.

5. Open Settings > Bluetooth.

6. If Bluetooth is off, click it to turn it on. You will see your Cricut Bluetooth device

7. Select your adapter/Bluetooth module name from the list (You will find the name of your adapter in your packaging materials.)

8. When prompted, type PIN 0000, then tap Pair.

9. Pairing is now complete.

10. Select Pair. When prompted, type the PIN code 0000 and select Pair

11. Pairing is now complete.

Note: The Mac computer will not always show "Connected" unless the program is communicating with the machine during a cut.

Setting up a Cricut Machine on a Mobile Device

1. Ensure that your Cricut Maker or Cricut Explore unit is turned on and within 10-15 feet of your mobile device. Whether you have a Cricut Explore or a Cricut Explore One, make sure that your Bluetooth Wireless Adapter is connected.
2. Open Settings > Bluetooth now.
3. If Bluetooth is gone, press it to turn it on.
4. Pick the name of your adapter/Bluetooth module from the list (you will find the name of your adapter in your packaging materials.)
5. When prompted, type PIN 0000, then select OK.
6. Pairing is now complete.

Note: The navigation menu can differ depending on the manufacturer of your Android device and the version of your Android device. Kindly refer to your Android System Manual for further support or email our Member Care Team using one of the choices below.

Tip: It's common for the Cricut Builder or the Cricut Explorer machines to appear in the Audio list. Whether you have multiple Cricut machines, you can use your system code to find the one you want to pair. It can be located at the bottom of the unit on the serial number tag.

CHAPTER 3 - EVERYTHING ABOUT DESIGN SPACE

CANVAS AREA

You'll do it from a window called CANVAS when you log in into your Cricut design space account and want to begin or edit a new project.

The Canvas Area in Cricut Design Room is in which you do all your editing before you break off your designs.

There are several icons, options, and stuff you need to do that you could feel confused Don't worry, I'm here to cheer and inspire you to continue. I'm here.

You're about to learn what Any ONE ICON is for in the Canvas area. To keep it in order and quick to grasp, we're going to split the canvas into four areas and four colors:

- Top Panel Yellow – Editing Area
- Left Panel Blue – Insert Area
- Right Panel Purple – Layers Panel
- Canvas Area Green

Top Panel Cricut Design Space

The top panel in the Design Room Canvas area is for editing and organizing the components in the canvas area. From this screen, you can select what sort of font you want to use; you can change fonts, match styles, and more!

Sub-panel #1 Name Your Project and Cut it

This sub-panel allows you to navigate from the Canvas to your profile, projects, and it also sends your completed projects to cut.

Toggle Menu   Project Name   My projects   Save Changes   Machine   Send to cut

Toggle Menu

When you press this key, another complete menu will be opened. This menu is a very handy one. But it isn't part of the Canvas, and that's why I'm not going to go into a lot of depth.

Apparently, from here on, you can go to your profile and update your picture.

There are some helpful and technological stuff you can do from this menu, such as calibrating your computer, blades, and upgrading the firmware – software – of your system.

You will also track your Cricut Access subscriptions, your account info, and more.

Project Name

All projects start with a *Untitled "Title," you can only name a project from the canvas area after you have put at least one part (Image, shape, etc.).

My Projects

When you click on my projects, you'll be guided to your library of things you've already made; that's awesome because maybe you might like to re-cut a project you've already created. So, you don't need to recreate the same project repetitively.

Save

This option will be enabled after you have placed one element in your canvas field. I strongly suggest that you save your project while you go. While this app is on the cloud, if your browser fails, your hard work is going on!

Maker – Explore (Machine)

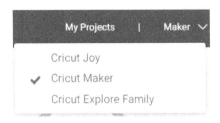

Based on the type of machine you have, you will need to pick either the Cricut Joy, the Builder or the Cricut Explore Machine; that's very essential because you will discover features on the Cricut Maker that are only available on that particular machine.

So, if you have a maker and you're planning the ON Explorer option, you won't be able to enable the resources that are for the maker.

The various choices are for the type of line.

Make it

When you are done uploading your files, and ready to cut click on Make it!

Down below is a screenshot of what you're about to do. Your designs are split into mats as per the colors of the group.

You may also maximize the amount of tasks to be cut from this window; this is perfect if you're trying to make more than one cut.

When you click on Make it. This is what you see

Subpanel #2 – Editing Menu

It's incredibly helpful, and it can help you edit, organize, and manage fonts and images in the Canvas Area.

Top Panel – Editing Menu

a. Undo & Redo

We commit errors even when we work. These little keys are a perfect way to repair them.

Click Undo anytime you build something that you don't like, or make a mistake.

Press Redo when you inadvertently delete something that you didn't intend to delete or alter.

b. Linetype and Fill

This choice would tell your machine what equipment and blades you're going to use.

Bear in mind that based on the machine you chose at the top of the window (Maker, Explore, or Joy) you would have different choices.

Linetype

This option will tell your machine when you are cutting your project, what tool you will be using. Right now, there are eight options (Cut, Draw, Score, Engrave, Deboss, Wave, Perf, and Foil).

If you have a Cricut Maker, all choices will be open; if you have an Explore, you will be able to Cut, Draw, Rate, and Foil; lastly, if you have a Cricut Joy, only Cut and Draw will be available.

Here is a more detailed description of each tool..

Cut

If you uploaded a JPEG or PNG image to the Canvas; "Cut" is the default line form that all of the components will have on the canvas; this means that when you click MAKE IT, your machine will remove those designs.

For the Cut option chosen, you will adjust the fill of the components, and at the end of the day, this converts into the various colors of the products you choose when you cut your designs.

You should do this with your Cricut if you want to write on your projects!

When you allocate this sort of line, you will be asked to pick either of the Cricut Pens that you have (You need specific pens, unless you have a 3rd party adapter). When you pick a custom style, the layers in your canvas area will be represented with the color of the pen you chose.

With this app, when you press Render it, the Cricut will write or draw instead of cutting it. Note: This choice does not color your designs.

Score

Score is a more effective version of the Score line on the left column. When you add this characteristic to a layer, all designs will be scored or dashed.

This time, when you're going to press Make it. Your Cricut is not going to slash, so it's going to score your materials.

You may require a score stylus or a score wheel for these kinds of projects. Bear in mind, nonetheless, that the wheel only fits with the Cricut Creator.

Engrave

Enable you to inscribe all kinds of materials. For example, you can create monograms on aluminum sheets or anodized aluminum to expose the silver underneath.

Deboss

This tip will drive the material in to produce stunning and informative designs. The debossing tip will encourage you to customize your designs to a whole new level.

Only imagine a stunning gift box with roses, hearts, stars, etc.!

Wave

Rather than cutting straight lines like a rotary or fine point cutter, this method can produce waved results on your final cuts.

Having curved lines in Design Space is pretty difficult, but this method is going to be useful if you like these kinds of effects.

Perf

The Perforation Blade is a tool that helps you to cut the products in small and even lines to produce flawless and crisp tear results like those you use in raffle tickets, coupons, tear-out cards, etc.

Foil (New)

Foil is the newest Cricut product that helps you to render beautiful foil details on your projects with the Cricut Foil Transfer Package.

While using this style of line, you have the option to select between good, medium and bold finishes.

Fill

The fill option is primarily used for printing and patterns.

It can only be allowed after you have Cut as a "linetype." **No Fill** means you're not going to print anything.

Print is by far one of the great features Cricut has, since it helps you to print your designs and then cut them; it's nice, and frankly, it's what motivates me to get a Cricut first.

When this Fill option is working, press Make it; first, you'll submit your files to your home printer, and then your Cricut will do all the heavy lifting. (Coupling)

Patterns is another incredible choice for the Print Form. Use Cricut's options, or upload your own; you can apply a template to almost any sort of layer.

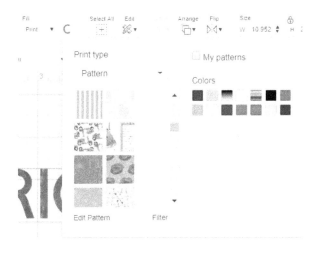

Fill for Print then Cut ONLY works with the Cricut Maker and any of the Explore Family Machines (it's not compatible with Cricut Joy).

c. Select All

If you need to transfer all of your objects inside the canvas area, you will struggle to pick them individually.

To pick all the items from the canvas, press Select All.

d. Edit

This icon will allow you to cut (remove from the canvas), copy (copy the same thing, leaving the original intact) and paste (insert copied or cut elements in the canvas area) items from the canvas.

The Edit button has a drop-down menu on it.

The Cut-and-Copy option will be enabled when you pick one or more items from the canvas area. The Paste choice will be activated until you have copied or cut something.

e. Align

If you have preview knowledge with other graphic design systems, you'll definitely know how to use this menu.

Align: This feature helps you to align all of your designs, and is enabled by choosing two or more items.

– **Align Left:** When this configuration is used, all the elements will be aligned to the left. The farthest element to the left would determine where all the other elements will pass.

– **Center Horizontal:** This choice would align the items horizontally; the text and photographs would be fully focused.

– **Align Right:** When you use this configuration, all of the elements will be aligned to the right. The farthest element to the right would determine where all the other elements will move.

– **Align Top:** All of your chosen designs will be aligned to the top of this option. The furthest element to the top will determine where all the other items will move.

– **Center Vertically:** This choice aligns the objects vertically. It's useful when you're dealing with columns, and you want them to be ordered and coordinated.

– **Align Bottom:** All of your chosen designs will be aligned to the bottom of this option. And the farthest element to the bottom will determine where all the other elements will move.

– **Center:** This is a really cool option. When you click on the "center" button, you are reorienting, both vertically and horizontally, one arrangement against the other; this is especially helpful when you try to center text with a shape like a square or a star.

Distribute: If you would like the same space between the elements, it's really time consuming to do it all on your own, and it's not 100% right. The Distribute icon is going to help you out of that. You should have at least three elements chosen to allow it.

– **Distribute Horizontally:** This button will scatter the components horizontally. The length of the distribution shall be calculated by the furthest left and right designs; this means that the products in the middle shall be separated between the most distant left and right designs.

– **Distribute Vertically:** This key will scatter the components vertically. The furthest top and bottom designs would decide the length of the distribution; this means that the products in the middle will be separated between the most distant top and bottom designs.

How to align in Cricut Design Space

f. Arrange

When you deal with different pictures, text, and templates, the latest creations you bring to the canvas will still be in front of you. Besides that, some of the components of the concept need to be in the back or in the front.

With the choice to arrange, you can organise the elements very quickly.

What are the choices that you'll get:

– **Send to back:** This will move the selected element all the way to the back.

– **Move Backward:** This option will move selected the item just one step back. So if you have a three-element design. It will be like the cheese in a cheese sandwich.

– **Move Forward:** This option will move the element just one step forward. Typically, you would use this option when you have four or more items you need to organize.

– **Sent to front:** This option will move the selected element all the way to the front.

g. Flip

If you need to reflect any of your designs in Cricut Design Space, this is a great way to do it.

There are 2 options:

– **Flip Horizontal:** This will represent your picture or your template horizontally. It's kind of like a mirror; it's useful when you're trying to build left and right patterns. Illustration: You are building some wings, and you already have the left side; with Flip, you can copy / paste the left wing, and voila! Now you've got all (left and right) wings!

– **Flip Vertical:** This is going to flip the designs vertically. It's sort of like you'd see your appearance in the water. If you want to create a shadow effect, that will be a fantastic choice for you.

h. Size

Anything that you build or type in Cricut Design Space has a size. You should change the size of the object to your own (when you click on it). Besides this, if you need an object to have a precise measurement, this choice would encourage you to do so.

Everything really critical is the little bolt. When you enhance or reduce the scale of a picture, the proportions will still be locked. By clicking on a tiny lock, you tell the machine you don't want to maintain the same measurements.

i. Rotate

Somewhat like size, rotating an aspect is something you can do from the canvas area very easily. Nevertheless, certain projects need to be adjusted to a particular angle. If this is the case for you, I suggest that you use this feature. Alternatively, you're going to waste too much time struggling to get an aspect angled the way you want it to be.

j. Position

This box tells you where the things are in the canvas area when you press on a particular template.

You can shift the components around by deciding where you want the element to be placed in the canvas areas. It's really helpful, but it's a more sophisticated platform.

k. Font

You can pick any font you want to use for your projects by clicking on this panel. You will filter them and check for them at the top of the browser.

If you have Cricut Control, you can use any of the fonts that have a little green A at the start of the font description.

l. Style

Once you pick your font, you have the option to change its form.

Some of the options you have:
– **Regular:** this is the default setting, and it won't change the appearance of your font.
– **Bold:** it will make the font thicker.
– **Italic:** it will tilt the font to the right.
– **Bold italic:** it will make the font thicker and tilt to the right.

m. Font Size, Letter & Line Space

Font Size: From here, you can adjust it manually. Typically, I just change the size of my fonts in the canvas area.

Letter Space: There is a significant distance between each letter in some fonts. This choice helps you to reduce the space between letters very easily. It's a really serious game-changer.

Line Space: This option would fix the line spacing in a paragraph; this is very helpful because often I am compelled to construct a single line of text because I am not comfortable with the line spacing.

n. Alignment

This Alignment differs from the other "alignment" I explained above. This option is for paragraphs.

These are the options you have:

– **Left:** Align a paragraph to the left
– **Center:** Align a paragraph to the center
– **Right:** Align a paragraph to the right.

o. Curve

This option will allow you to make extra creative with your text!

With this feature, you can curve your text—the easiest way to practice it is by playing with a little slider.

As you move the slider to the left, the text curves upwards; and when you move it to the right, the text curves inwards.

.

p. Advance

Advance is the last option on the Edit panel.

So, do not be confused by the name of the drop-down menu. When you understand what all the options are about, you'll find they're not that hard to use.

− Ungroup to Letters: This option would allow you to split each letter into a single layer (I'll elaborate more about layers below); use this if you're planning to change each character.

− Ungroup to Lines: This option is incredible and will enable you to split a paragraph on individual lines. Type the paragraph, then press ungroup to the row, and there you have it; a new line that you can change now.

– **Ungroup to Layers:** This is the most complicated of all these options. This option is only available for Multi-Layer fonts; these types of fonts are only available for individual transactions and for Cricut Access.

A multi-layer font is a type of font with more than one layer; these fonts are perfect if you want to have some shadow or color around it.

What if you want a multi-layer font and you don't want the layer to be added? Only pick your text and then press Ungroup to separate layers on each layer.

Left panel – Attach Forms, Pictures and More

Left Panel

With the top panel (which I just described in detail) you're going to edit all the templates.

So where are they all coming from? They all come from the left panel of the Cricut Concept Room Panel.

This panel is all about adding forms, pictures, designs ready to be sliced, and more. From here, you're going to add all the stuff you're going to cut.

The Panel has seven choices:

– **New:** to create and replace a new project in the canvas area.

– **Templates:** this allows you to have a guide on the types of things you are going to cut.– - **Projects:** Add ready to cut projects from Cricut Access.

– **Images:** Pick single images from Cricut Access, and cartridges to create a project.

– **Text:** Click here to add text on your canvas area.

– **Shapes:** Insert all kinds of shapes on the canvas.

– **Uploads:** Upload your images and cut files to the program.

There is also something basic which you need to acknowledge in this panel; whether you have Cricut Access, Cricut Images, ready to cut programs, and Cricut fonts cost money. If you need them, you're going to have to pay before you cut off your project.

Now, we've had a little taste of what it was all about on this panel. Let's see what transpires when you press on each of these keys.

a. New

When you click on NEW, even if you're still working on a project, you'll get an alert at the top of the screen inquiring whether or not you want to modify the project.

When you plan to change your project, ensure you save all the modifications from the new project; otherwise, you'll miss all the hard work. Once you save, a new, empty canvas will open for you to get started.

b. Templates

Templates help you illustrate and see if your idea works on a particular surface. This element, I find, is just out of this universe.

If you choose to customize fashion pieces, this app is wonderful since you can pick sizes and various styles of clothes. Plus, they also have a number of different types that you can pick from.

Note: templates are just for you to visualize. Nothing will be cut when you finish designing and send your project to be cut.

c. Projects

If you want to cut right now, so Projects is where you want to go! After you have chosen your project, you can configure it; or press make it, and follow the cutting guidelines.

d. Images

Images are great when you put together your own projects; with them, you can add an additional touch and personality to your art.

You can search by keyword, highlighted groups, subjects, people, locations, times, etc.

Cartridges are a collection of images that you need to buy separately; some of them come with Cricut Control, some of them not. (Brands such as Disney, Sesame Street, Hello Kitty, etc. are not part of Cricut Access)

Under "Highlighted Categories" Cricut has FREE pictures to be cut every week.

Whenever you click under either category, a more efficient filter will appear. You can limit the quest even more with this filter.

e. Text

Whenever you want to type in the Canvas Area, you will need to press Text; then a tiny window that says "Add Text Here" will appear on the canvas.

f. Shapes

It's important to be able to use shapes! With them, you can build simple, less complex, and (also) beautiful designs.

There are nine shapes that you can pick from:

- Square
- Triangle
- Pentagon
- Hexagon
- Star
- Octagon
- Heart

The last option is not a shape, but a marvelous and efficient tool called Score Line. You can create folds and score your materials with this option.

If you want to build boxes or enjoy all about creating a card, the Score Line would be your best friend!

g. *Upload*

Last, but not least!

You can upload your files and photos with this option. The internet is packed with them; there are hundreds of bloggers making projects for free.

Right Panel – Learn All about Layers

Layers reflect any single feature or design in the canvas area.

Assume of it as clothing; as you get ready, you have several layers that make up your outfit; and based on the day, or the time of year, your outfit can be basic or complicated.

Thus, on a cold day, the garments will be shorts, trousers, top, scarf, sock, boots, gloves, etc., and for a day at the beach, you will have just one coat, the Bathing Suit!

The same thing happens with the design; based on the size of the project you're working on, you're going to have multiple layer styles that make up your whole project.

a. Group, Ungroup, Duplicate and Delete

These settings can make your life simpler as you move stuff around the canvas field, so make sure you play around with them.

Group: Tap here to see the group layers. This setting is useful because you have multiple layers that make up a complicated architecture.

Let's just claim that you're working on an elephant. Quite definitely (even if this is an SVG or cut file) the elephant will be made up of various layers (body, eyes, legs, trunk, etc.); if you want to add additional shapes and text; most likely, you'll be pushing the elephant around the canvas field a lot.

So, by grouping all the elephant layers together, you can make sure that it remains ordered and nothing gets out of place as you pass them across the canvas.

Ungroup: This function would ungroup any layers you pick from the canvas region or layers panel. Use this option if you need to modify (size, font style, etc.) a specific group feature or sheet.

Duplicate: This option will duplicate any layers or designs you have selected on the layers panel or canvas.

Delete: This option will delete any elements you have selected on the canvas or layers panel.

b. Linetype/Fill

Every item on the Layers Panel will show what Linetype or Fill you are using (Cut, Write, Score, Perf, Wavy, Print, etc.).

c. Layer Visibility

The tiny eye that emerges on each sheet of the layer panel reflects the visibility of the pattern. If you're not sure if the feature looks fine, rather than removing it, press the little eye to cover the item. Note: The eye will have a cross mark when you cover an object.

d. Blank Canvas

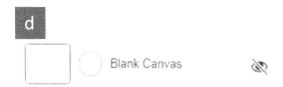

This "layer" helps you to adjust the color of the canvas; whether you're looking to see how a certain style looks with a different color. The strength of this setting is activated as you use it along with the

Templates tool so you can change the color and the design choices on your own.

e. *Slice, Weld, Attach, Flatten and Contour*

This tools that you see here are extremely important! But make sure you're learning them to excellence. I'm not going into a lot of depth on them because they merit tutorials on their own.

Conversely, I'm going to give you a short explanation of what they're all about by using the graphic below.

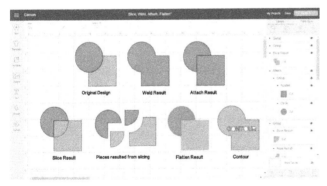

Slice, Weld, Attach, Flatten, and Contour Info-Graphic

As you can see from the graphic, the original concept is a pink circle with a teal rectangle. Now let's see what's going to happen when I use all these choices.

Slice

The cutting tool is ideal for cutting shapes, text and other components in various styles.

When I picked all shapes and tapped on the slice, you will see that the original file was all sliced up; to show you what the final result was, I copied and pasted the "slice result" and then split all the bits that came out of the slicing.

Weld

The welding tool allows you to combine two or more shapes in one.

Attach

Attach works like grouping layers, but it's more powerful.

Flatten

This tool is additional support for Print then Cut Fill settings; when you adjust the fill from no fill to print, it only applies to one sheet. What if at the moment you try to do it in different shapes?

When you're finished with your template, pick the layers you want to print together as one, and then press flatten.

When you're through with your template (you can't undo this until you've completed your project), pick the layers you want to print together as a whole, and then press flatten.

In this case, the feature is a print, then a cut pattern, and that's why it doesn't display a black edge (where the blade is going through) anymore.

Contour

The Contour tool helps you to cover unused template parts which will only be enabled if the form or design has components that should be left out.

f. Color Sync

Color Sync is the last option on the layers panel.

Each color on your canvas area reflects a different color of the paint. If your template has several shades of yellow or blue, are you sure you need them?

If you need just one shade of yellow, just like this scenario. Only press and drag the tone you want to get rid of and lower it to the one you want to hold.

Canvas Area

The canvas area is where you can see all of the layouts and items. It's very straightforward and easy to use!

a. Canvas Grid and Measurements

The canvas area is separated by a grid; this is perfect because every little square you see on the grid makes you imagine the cutting pad. In the end, this will help you optimize your space.

You can adjust the dimensions from inches to cm and turn the grid on and off when you press on the top panel and then choose Settings. (You can see this toggle menu " at the start of this tutorial)

The window would open up with all the options available.

Turn the Grid off and on

b. Selection

Whenever you pick one or more layers, the selection is blue, and you can change it from all four corners.

The "red x" is used to erase the layers. The upper right corner will enable you to rotate the picture (although if you need a specific angle, I suggest you to use the rotate tool on the editing menu).

The lower right button of the pick, "Small Lock," holds the size equivalent as you raise or reduce the size of your layer. You are now going to get varying amounts by tapping on it.

c. *Zoom In and Out*

Last but not least of all. If you want to see in a larger or smaller scale (without changing the actual dimensions of the designs), you can do this by clicking the "+" and "-" signs in the lower left corner of the canvas.

That's it – You are not a beginner anymore!

CHAPTER 4 - WHAT IS CRICUT ACCESS?

Cricut Access is a subscription-based program that gives you unrestricted access to more than 50,000+ images, 1000 projects and fonts. What is this? How's it distinct from De-signSpace? What's used here? What's the right value for you? Read on to learn more.

There are two distinct degrees of preference. Each standard can be charged on a monthly or annual subscription basis (the yearly having a lower rate over monthly payments).

Monthly Membership:
Through the Monthly Subscription you will have access to over 400 fonts that are ready to be used with your Cricut computer, access to the Priority Member Support Line for quick assistance whenever you need it, unrestricted use of over 30,000 Cricut images, with exclusive templates, 10 per cent discount for all approved fonts, images and ready-to-make creations, and 10 per cent on all product sales on Cricut.com.

Annual Membership:
The next step to membership is the annual membership. The yearly membership is much like the monthly membership, but is charged at a reduced rate on an annual basis. Through the yearly subscription, you will have access to more than 400 fonts that are ready to be used on your Cricut computer, access to the Priority Member support line for quicker assistance when you need it, unrestricted use of more than 30,000 Cricut images, with

exclusive templates, 10% savings for all approved fonts, images and ready-to-make creations, and 10% off all merchandise orders on Cricut.com.

Premium Membership:

The Premium Membership is the highest level of Cricut Access available. Premium Mem-bership allows you access to more than 400 fonts that are ready to be used on your Cricut machine, access to the Priority Membership Line for quicker support when you need it, unrestricted use of more than 30,000 Cricut images, plus unique templates, 10% discounts on all approved fonts, images and ready-to-make creations, and 10% off all orders on Cricut.com, along with all purchases on Cricut.com.

CHAPTER 5 - CRICUT ACCESS FAQ

What's the difference between Cricut Access and Cricut Design Space?
Cricut Access and Cricut Design Room are two distinct artifacts. Design Space is a software that you use to design your project. Cricut Access is a subscription-based program that allows you access to additional designs inside Design Space (and other perks).

Do I need Cricut Access?
If you plan to buy more than a few designs a month, or if you order items from Cricut's website on a daily basis, you'll want to join.

How do I know if an object is contained in my Cricut Access subscription?
:

If the Cricut Access subscription contains an image, project or font, the top corner will be a green 'a.'

The Green Cricut Access banner will display whether or not you have a Cricut Access account. You'll find it says "Subscribed" and you can do it without paying anything extra if you have an Entry account. If you don't have an Entry account, you can always buy the sketches, but there would be a separate fee.

CAN I USE YOUR DISCOUNT CODE TO GET A DISCOUNT ON CRICUT ACCESS?

No. But you CAN use it after you have Access and combine it with your Access discount

WHAT IS THE DIFFERENCE BETWEEN CRICUT ACCESS AND DESIGN SPACE? DO I NEED CRICUT ACCESS TO USE DESIGN SPACE?

Cricut Access is an exclusive membership package that offers incentives for free and approved designs at a reduced price, such as access to Cricut images, fonts and projects. Cricut Design Room is a free app that you use to build or upload designs and cut them to your Cricut. Both users of the Cricut Explore kin, Maker and Joy must download and use the free Cricut Concept Space app.

I DIDN'T SIGN UP FOR MY FREE TRIAL, CAN I STILL USE THE FREE TRIAL?

Yes, you can still use your free trial for Cricut Access. Here are the steps to do that:

1. Open the Cricut Design Space app on your computer or device.

2. Click on three horizontal lines in the top left corner on your desktop, or the circle with your initials in the top left on the app, to view the Profile drop down.

3. Click on "Cricut Access"

4. A new screen will pop up which will show you if you have a free trial available and walk you through the process to use it.

DO I NEED TO HAVE CRICUT ACCESS TO USE MY CRICUT MACHINE?

No. Cricut Access is completely optional.

DOES CRICUT ACCESS WORK FOR MY LEGACY CRICUT MACHINE (CRICUT PERSONAL, CREATE, EXPRESSION, EXPRESSION 2, MINI, CAKE, CAKE MINI AND IMAGINE)

Apparently, no. Legacy machines are not compliant with the Cricut Design Space system. Legacy machines, apart from the Cricut Mini, have been used as discrete machines after the shutdown of the Cricut Craft Space.

SHOULD I GET CRICUT ACCESS?

Cricut Access is a perfect time and money saver for regular craftsmen. If you want to use various images and fonts, particularly licensed images and projects, you'll find that Cricut Access is a good addition to your work. Also it saves you time because you don't need to browse the internet in search of images or fonts. Also, if you buy Cricut.com goods, the savings could add up and pay for themselves!

HOW DO I KNOW IF I HAVE CRICUT ACCESS ALREADY?

If you are signed in to your Cricut account either via the website, Design Space Desktop or one of the Design Space applications, you can click to view My Account. Prefer Cricut Access from the drop-down menu. The pop-up screen will let you know if you are already enrolled and when the subscription will be renewed.

DO I HAVE TO LIVE IN THE US TO SUBSCRIBE?

No, but not all of the plans are available in all regions. The choices of the Cricut Access Standard differ based on where the Cricut customer lives.

- **Cricut Access Premium** is only offered to users in the US and Canada.
- US, UK and Canada Cricut users can subscribe to monthly or yearly Access Standard.

- Users in all other countries can subscribe to the monthly Access Standard option via the Cricut Design Space app for iOS or Android.

HOW CAN I TELL IF A DESIGN IS INCLUDED IN CRICUT ACCESS?

While you are in the Design space, if you see an image, font or project with a small green flag and the letter "a" in the top left corner that identifies the item as one that is included in the Cricut Access subscription. If you have a Cricut Access membership, instead of displaying the price at the bottom of the picture box, it would say "Subscribed."

You can also view Cricut Access designs by choosing Cricut Access in the filter options.

You can see a complete list of the images included in Cricut Access at https://help.cricut.com/hc/en-us/articles/360009424614-Cartridge-Handbooks

WHAT HAPPENS IF I USE A CRICUT ACCESS IMAGE IN A DESIGN, THEN LATER DON'T SUBSCRIBE? CAN I STILL USE THE DESIGN I MADE?

Photos, fonts or projects that you have already used for free as part of your Cricut Access membership would be accessible at a discount if you are no longer a member. When you press the Make It button, you will be asked to pay the bill.

CAN I SELL ITEMS I CREATE USING CRICUT ACCESS DESIGNS?

Kindly direct to **Cricut's Angel Policies** for an overview of how you will be able to sell products that integrate Cricut Access photos, fonts or patterns. Please notice that the Cricut Angel Policy is subject to modification.

IF I DON'T SUBSCRIBE TO CRICUT ACCESS, CAN I STILL BUY THE IMAGES?

Yes, all images, fonts and projects are accessible at a one-time price. The price is seen at the bottom left of the preview box as you click through all of the pictures. After you buy the file, it's up to you to use it as much as you like, as long as it's still accessible via Cricut Design Space.

HOW DO I CHANGE MY CRICUT SUBSCRIPTION OR CANCEL?

Cricut Access subscriptions are regularly renewed. You will handle this auto-renewal at https://cricut.com/customer/account. If you've signed up with your iOS or Android app, you'll need to change or cancel your subscription via iTunes or Google Play. Read more on how to cancel at Cricut.com.

If you want to upgrade from Regular to Premium, just go buy the Premium and, after it's over, go to your subscriptions and cancel your monthly package. If you prefer to optimize your time, wait for the last day of your monthly contract (the day before it is renewed) and then purchase Premium—just make sure you never cancel your monthly plan. This is how I did it, and it went well.

IF I CANCEL CRICUT ACCESS, CAN I SUBSCRIBE AGAIN?

Yes, If you cancel, your account will stay valid until the conclusion of the current billing period. If you wish to restart your Access subscription at any moment, you can do so by signing in to your Cricut account on the website and buying the Access subscription you want from https://cricut.com/en us/cricut-access.html. You can also buy via the Cricut Design Space app by watching My Account drop down and then taping Cricut Access.

CHAPTER 6 - CRICUT PROBLEMS AND SOLUTIONS

The Cricut cutting machine is a wonderful technology. It lets us make so many wonderful things. Yet occasionally the cuts aren't as smooth as we would like, and it's not really clear why or what we can do to correct it. But today, I'm going to go over the five items you need to pay attention to when you cut your Cricut Explore or Cricut Maker. With this, you can solve almost every problem with Cricut cutting and make those perfect, clean cuts!

The five aspects you need to pay attention to are your Pad, Sword, Cloth, Atmosphere, and PATTERN. And that's the same sequence with which I go while I'm troubleshooting the issue of cutting, too.

CRICUT CUTTING PROBLEM SOLUTION #1: USE A STICKY MAT

Your Cricut mat needs to be sticky enough to allow clean cuts. So if your cuts aren't clean, the first thing you're going to do is change your mat. Typically, I turn to a different or newer mat, and it fixes my problem immediately. If you can't afford a new mat, you can try cleaning your mat with a dishwashing soap and leaving it to air dry to make it stickier. A sticky mat will make a significant difference.

CRICUT CUTTING PROBLEM SOLUTION #2: USE A CLEAN, SHARP BLADE

You have to ensure that your Cricut blade is clean and smooth. I do so by taking a sheet of aluminum foil and balling it up like that. Then I detach the blade from its housing, compress the plunger, and stick it inside and out of the aluminum ball Cautiously over and over—maybe 50 times. This cleans any residue off the blade, such as fragments of paper or vinyl that may be sticking to the blade, and it even appears to sharpen. (It may not really be sharpening, but it works!) This method works with the Fine-Point and Deep-Point Knives.

If the concern is not that the blade doesn't cut all the way though, but rather that it slices TOO MUCH, it could be because you're using the wrong blade. Check the packaging—you need to use the Premium Fine-Point (German Carbide) blade with Cricut Explorer and Cricut Maker. Out of their packaging, the Luxury Fine-Point Blades can be defined by the colour of the caps, either WHITE or RED. Don't use the gray cap blades—they are intended for older Cricut machines and are too long for Cricut Explores and Creators.

CRICUT CUTTING PROBLEM SOLUTION #3: USE QUALITY MATERIALS

Your content, too, will make a significant difference in how it slices. For eg, not all of the paper is produced equal. If the fibers in the paper are thinner or shorter, as you usually see in poorer quality paper, you'll get more tears. So, even after using a sticky mat and a new razor, if the paper doesn't seem to be cutting properly, the paper itself could be the culprit. There's been a lot of times where I've had a problem, and then I've moved to a new paper just to make it run properly. Cricut paper is of good quality, so are the recollections. Keep out of the Park Lane brand. So, until you give up on the idea, try a new paper!

CRICUT CUTTING PROBLEM SOLUTION #4: CHECK YOUR SETTINGS

It's very critical that you have the right material settings. To do this on the Cricut Explore, just spin the Custom dial and you'll be asked to pick your content before you cut it. (Note that the Manufacturer does not have a dial—you are on "customer settings" by default.) And if it still doesn't seem to help, aim to raise the strength of the cut. That's why I've almost always got "more" strain on my cuts—it always seems to help me get those clean cuts.

CRICUT CUTTING PROBLEM SOLUTION #5: CHECK YOUR PATTERN

Not all patterns are going to be cut neatly. The smaller and more complex and complicated they are, the harder it would be to cut them. They're just too little often. So, if that's an alternative, you can try getting them bigger. If this doesn't work or is not an alternative, you can try setting the material to Complicated Cuts if you're cutting cardstock. Or consider setting the washi tape while you're cutting vinyl. None of these are sure to succeed, but it's worthwhile. At the end of the day, any pattern can just be too small or intricate to be cut without any problems. This doesn't mean that all is lost, even so you will still be able to cut it and clean it with a scissor or a knife later.

CHAPTER 6 - CRICUT MANTENANCE

Cleaning the Cricut Machines
- Gently clean the outside panels with a wet rag.
- Dry instantly any residual moisture with a chamois or other soft fabric.

- Do not use chemical or alcohol-based cleaners (including, but not limited to, acetone, benzene and carbon tetrachloride) on the unit. Scratchy cleaners and washing machines can also be avoided. Do not immerse the system or any of its parts in water.
- Keep away from food and liquids, try not to consume or drink when operating the computer.
- Keep in a dry, dust-free spot.
- Avoid intense heat or cold, do not leave the unit in the car where excessive heat will melt or damage plastic parts.
- Do not subject to direct sunlight for some lengthy period of time.

Cleaning Your Cricut Mat

A Cricut mat somewhat lacks its function when the surface has become imprecise and is unable to make accurate cuts.

You'll know when it's time to vacuum the mat, when the fabrics don't hold like they used to, or when the surface is sticky, and when soft particles get in the way.

Cleaning the mat would not involve the use of advanced materials. In addition, some of them can be found in most homes and in cleaning cabinets.

Step 1. Light Cleaning

The first thing you want to do is whip out the reliable plastic scraper you want to order from Cricut. If not, there would be a related hard plastic scraper. Run the substance carefully and methodically over the surface to remove minor particles. Do this a few times before continuing to the next stage.

Step 2. Baby Wipes and Lint Roller

Consider this or not, baby wipes are the best cleaning mates for your Cricut pad, since they are moist and soft enough to leave your mat unscathed. But here's the thing, not all baby wipes can be used to clean Cricut mats! Select one which is chlorine and alcohol-free, or risk losing the stickiness of the mat permanently.

Run the wipe over the surface carefully, and make sure you cover everything in a straight line. You can be tempted to hit the nail varnish remover, but it's safer to be careful than sorry. Baby wipes and lint rollers, and even good old-fashioned soap and water, can work wonders to make your Cricut mat look revived and ready to be cut.

Lint rollers are used to execute two tasks. One, you will strip away the stubborn matter that isn't going to come with rubber scrapers and baby wipes. Two, the rollers are sticky and can transfer some of their stickiness to the surface of the mat. Only a one-two mix of baby wipes and lint rollers is appropriate to eliminate a slight build-up.

Step 3. Soap & Water

Once in a while, you'll want to wash your Cricut mat with a container filled with soapy water.

Enable the mat to soak for around 5 to 10 minutes before it is removed. If there is something that isn't going to wash off, just use a small brush to scrub with warm water. You may also use a sponge, a Magic Eraser or an adhesive remover for specific residue. Only make sure you read the guidelines that come with the cleaning tool. Yeah, and you're definitely going to have to restart your mat later.

Step 4. Air Dry

When you're comfortable with how clean your Cricut mat feels, it's time to hang it to dry.

Wait until the mat is fully dried before using it again. The use of a towel, tissue or paper would be counter-intuitive since little pieces adhere to the surface and reduce total efficacy.

How to Restore the Stickiness of Cricut Mats

Is your Cricut mat lost its stickiness, and now you can't be as accurate as you want it to be?

Don't worry-there are a variety of ways you can get it sticky and usable again.

You're going to need an adhesive spray, either a sticky spray or a repositionable adhesive for this one. They are all sold in specialty art shops and online retailers and are relatively inexpensive. Bear in mind that each product can have different guidelines for use, so be sure to read them before all else.

Any of the uncommon re-stick products that you can use in a hurry include a quilting spray, re-positionable glue sticks, and scrapbooking glue. If all the materials are ready, let's continue.

Cover the edges of your Cricut mat with a mask or a painter's tape. It's crucial not to make the edges sticky because they're not going to damage the cutting machine.

Step 1 – Remove the residual stickiness to ensure that the adhesive spray covers the mat uniformly. Apply the simple rubbing alcohol or Goo Gone to the floor, and go over it with a scraper.

Step 2 – Spray or spread the sticky spray gently and cover the surface of the Cricut mat uniformly. Certain items would need you to brush a few times, whereas others will only perform their magic by making contact. Again, follow the directions on the package for the better performance.

Step 3 – Enable the adhesive to rest and bind properly to the surface of the mat. After about 15 to 20 minutes, gently cut the tape from the sides and check the finished product. Your Cricut mat should be fresh and ready for action!

Conclusion

Cleaning your Cricut mat is necessary so that you can use accurate methods without thinking about soil, dust or lint getting in the way. We will suggest getting care of your mat surface and clean it periodically using the above methods.

In addition, repairing the Cricut mat helps the material to slip uniformly through the cutting machine and to remain intact throughout the process.

CHAPTER 6 - GETTING STARTED ON YOUR FIRST PROJECT

This chapter is going to be an exciting part for you, because we're going to learn about the various projects you can make, and they're all fast. Before you start working with this unit, it's best to start with something small so that you don't waste materials and so that you don't use the wrong blades or objects. Know, if you're using the wrong razor, the machine can tell you about it. This is really useful anytime you need to make sure you're doing the right project. Projects don't have to be too complex. This is the only justification for irritation you don't need. Here's the thing: as you get more experienced and used to the machine, tougher projects are fantastic, but think about it like this: if you try to learn anything different, odds are (in most cases) that you're not astounding right away. Training is fine. Start the little one and gradually build up.

Getting Ready for Your First Project

- The first step you have to do is log in to your Cricut.com account.

- Then you'll need to look at the "Design" button in the right corner.

- At the start of a new project in the Design Space app, you can see a window that says, "Canvas." That's the screen where you'll have to get your design ready before you cut it. You'll see a number of different panels for editing and scaling or modifying fonts, and it's pretty easy to get around each one and see what they're doing. The first panel will help you to explore your canvas and submit your finished designs to be cut.

- You will need to ensure that you have lined up the design choices for the machine you have.

- Don't set your Explore to Maker, or vice versa, because it would make you unable to function properly.

- The Edit menu is incredibly helpful as it allows you arrange or organise fonts and images on the screen, and it's easy to find, but it also helps you to edit it to make sure it's exactly the way you want it to be.

- You're going to make mistakes when you're practicing, and there are two little keys that have the potential to fix that for you. It gives either a delete button or a redo button. You should press the undo button if you've built something you don't want.

- Press the redo button anytime you unintentionally delete something that you know you really like, so you accidentally delete it.

- You also have a line form and fill option. Through these choices, you'll be able to tell your machine what equipment and blades you're going to use. Bear in mind that based on the machine you've already chosen, you'll have various options. A perfect example is to note that the Explorer only cuts three blades, and the Builder has six blades.

- The line style option tells the machine where you're going to cut and what instrument you're going to use, as well as giving you seven choices.

- If you have a Builder, any alternative will be open, but if you have an Adventurer, you will have only three choices available rather than seven. The first choice you're going to have is the cut.

- The cut option is the norm, and any object on your canvas has this option. This ensures that as you click to make it, the machine will cut the designs for you. When you have picked a cut, you will change the inside of the components and transform them into various colors of the products you are going to use.

- If you want to sketch your plans, you can do this when you allocate them. You'll be asked to pick some of the pens you've got (you will need very specific pens to do this). When choosing a specific template, the layers in the canvas region will be represented with the color of the pen you have selected. Rather than cutting as you want to make it, it's going to draw. Your designs are not colored by this choice.

- You can have individual choices for blades (such as perforation, wavy, and knife) while the fill option is used for patterns and printing.

- The Edit icon will give you choices for organising your project as well as adjusting the scale, location and design of the project. Mind, though, that your left panel is primarily used to insert pictures or shapes. The panels would have the opportunity to adopt a checklist for the planning of tasks and new models.

- The correct panel is for layering. These layers are symbolic of the design or of some feature on the canvas. An example that makes it simpler is to picture yourself wearing a suit or a dress. You have a sheet below the top layer. It is related to the idea of project style. Layering also helps you to adjust the hue of the canvas. You will have the ability to sync, flatten, and group and also ungroup.

Tips and Strategies for Your First Project

Here are several practical ideas and techniques to use before beginning the first project:

- If you group or ungroup, you are grouping layers or ungrouping layers, which is quite easy. If you have a repeat, this choice will reproduce any layers you want and choose to reproduce. Delete just means that you're deleting something that you've determined you don't want to touch.

- You have the exposure of the sheet and the line form fill, which we've already been through. Visibility of the sheet basically means that you are looking at the visibility of the design. The symbol is supposed to look like a tiny eyeball. By clicking on a layer and moving it, you can move a specific template under or above a blank canvas.

- The layer helps you to change the color of the canvas. You're still going to get a wheel, attach, flatten, contour, or slice. These tools are extremely valuable because they will allow you to transform your project and move it to the next level. The cutting tool is ideal for cutting shapes or other components in various styles.

- The welding tool helps you to fuse two or three forms into one. Attachment functions like grouping layers, but it's more effective by providing the opportunity to sit in place.

- The flatten alternative means that you pick the layers that you want to print together as a whole, and then press flatten. The feature will become a print, and the template will be cut.

- -Contouring helps you to cover unnecessary concept pieces so that you don't get a layout with noticeable errors.

- Color sync is the next choice you've got. Every color on your canvas is a different material. If your style has several colors, you might drag the tone you want to get rid of and remove the tones you want to hold.

- Your canvas area will have a grid and dimensions, and will allow you to pick and zoom in and out. Through doing this, you're going to be able to see what you can for your canvas, and you're going to be able to get the pictures on the canvas precisely as you want. Until you've gotten used to all these aspects, it should be quick and fast to do your project.

Loading Materials

When you need materials, you'll be instructed and prompted to load each mat accurately and then pick up your material, so you know what blade you need for score and depth. In specific, the Builder takes the guesswork out of these moves. When you're doing a project with these machines, it's as easy as understanding this: follow the choices on the computer. You will make things like these ideas right here with these machines:

Children's clothes

- Patterns for sewing

- Cuts in leather

- Making jewelry

- Cutting into the fabric (remember, the Maker cuts three hundred!)

- Magnets

- Homemade cards

- Quilting

Such projects are simpler to do with the Maker machine, however if you check the list below, there are projects that both series will do. This is so the Maker can do all the things Explore can do, plus more:

- Stencils (look in the tips chapter for how to make these cheaper)

- Clothing

- Gift tags

- Homemade wrapping paper

- Flowers

- Baby clothing

- Wedding decorations

- Wrapping paper

- Journals

- Tumblers (personalized)

- Dog clothing

- Decor for the house

- Invitations

- Coloring pages (great for parents with children or even adults)

Handmade with Love Tags

The first project we're going to describe is the gift tags. The explanation is because they are a perfect complement to every gift, or if you own a company, they bring a personal touch, and consumers enjoy it because it shows that you care. You'll find hundreds of various saying tags in Design Space, and that's what you're going to do here.

Materials needed

- Whichever Cricut machine you have chosen to purchase

- An active Design Space account

- A ready-made Design Space tag project. For this project, we'll assume that you've picked a tag that says "Handmade with love" to suit the company example we've used above.

- Vinyl and cardstock

- Your choice of a glitter pen color Step

Step 1

The first step you have to do is ensure you adopt the instructions to draw each layer and then cut each layer as the project demands.

Step 2

Glue the two layers of paper together before aligning the tag opening at the top of the tag.

Step 3

Attach the vinyl you've picked and burn it. The explanation why this is necessary is that you need to be sure that the vinyl is adhered to properly and accurately.

Step 4

Choose what you want to add to the tag hole. If you like, you can use a rope, a twine, or something more festive.

This is what you need for your first project. Simple and enjoyable, but the best thing is that it can be changed to fit for any kind of saying. If you don't like "Handmade with Love," you may want to consider the following suggestions for a saying:

- Thank you

- Homemade gift

- All-natural

- Made especially for you

- Handmade for you

- From the heart of (here you would write your name)

- Enjoy

- Organic

- Happy holidays

- Happy birthday

Or any other similar expressions. If you have a business you could put your business name at the bottom.

Handmade Card

They're super easy to make, and they don't take a lot of time. What you need to do is reap the benefits of your design room. Cards are a wonderful thing to master, so you can make use of them for every holiday or gift. All likes a card because it's a simple, meaningful touch. Many people enjoy homemade presents, too, and you should make them see that you have done this yourself and that you care for it.

Materials needed

- Whatever Cricut machine you have purchased

- An active Design Space account

- 65 lb. of 8.5 by 11-inch cardstock

Step 1

Go to your Design Space and pick a card project ready and then, for any shot you want, click on "Upload picture."

Step 2

Pick the file you intend to use. When it emerges on your window, press the Save button.

Step 3

Tap where it says, "Lately uploaded pictures." Click "Insert Images" and then click "Continue."

Step 4

Set your dial to cardstock.

Step 5

Place your cardstock onto your mat. Click the Go button to start cutting. Since cards are a two-sheet job, you'll need to load another mat with another card sheet onto your machine. Your Design Space will show you the color you need to cut next. You will be done here if you wish. Besides that, we're going to go a bit deeper and teach you how to cut a gift card slot with an extra touch:

1.Upload your image and place it on your canvas with the steps above.

2.Click on the image that is on your canvas and press the button that says, "Ungroup."

3.Click "Shapes/square."

4.Press and drag your square over the card segment where you want your slot to be.

5. Hold it down the shift key before pressing the square and the card segment below to pick both.

6.Click the weld button in the lower right corner. Now you've had a fantastic job that you've done and you've had some success on the machine. The best part is that you've got a perfect way to design cards for every reason, and the best part? Like bookmarks, you've got countless possibilities for suggestions.

Rugrats T-Shirt

Everybody loved the Rugrats in the 90s, and now you can put back your passion with a homemade T-Shirt with your favorite character. The directions on this don't take long, and this is a fun project that will take your art to a different level as well.

Materials needed

The Explore Air or the Maker

An iron

A small piece of fabric or linen cloth

T-Shirts A

Rugrats file (SVG file)

Supplies from the Cricut Company, which are these:

-Access membership

-The standard cutting mat

-Weeder

-Scissors

-An iron-on lite (vinyl)

An iron-on glitter

Step 1

Open your design in the Design Space and choose the color scheme you want to use.

Step 2

Attach your images to cut.

Step 3

Place your vinyl onto the cutting mat, and be sure that the shiny side is down. Load your mat into the machine.

Step 4

Click the "Go" button to start the cutting process. Make sure that your image is mirrored. You will have to check the box that says mirror image.

Step 5

Weed your cut design.

Step 6

Repeat the process with the different pieces of your images using different vinyl pieces to add color.

Step 7

Place the image on the shirt how you want it to look.

Step 8 Iron.

Be careful.

Step 9

Focus on the corners of your design.

Step 10

It should peel easily.

These shirts are a perfect way for you to be creative and have fun. Is your kid like unicorns or superheroes? You should do it, too! With the Cricut computer, you are constrained by your own imagination. There are thousands of styles you can use for T-Shirts, from movies, comics, anime, your favorite childhood characters, and everything else you can imagine, like pet creatures, quotations, and whatever else!

Glitter Tumbler

Materials needed

- Painters tape

- Mod podge and paintbrush

- Epoxy

- Glitter

- Stainless steel tumbler

- Spray paint

- Vinyl

- Wet/dry sandpaper

- Gloves

- Plastic cup

- Measuring cup

- Rubbing alcohol

Step 1

Tape off the top and bottom of the tumbler

Step 2

Make sure to seal them well enough that you know paint won't get on either.

Step 3

Spray paint twelve inches away from your tumbler in an area that is well ventilated. Make sure that the items you used are approved and will not make you sick.

Step 4

Once your tumbler is dry from the paint you have used, you can add the glitter.

Step 5

This will make a mess, so have something under it to catch the glitter. Put the mod podge in a small container. Use a flat paintbrush to put it on.

Step 6

Take the lid off and rotate the cup, adding glitter. Make sure it's completely covered.

Step 7

Make sure that the excess glitter will come off before removing the tape and letting it dry.

Step 8

When dry, take a flat brush that is clean and stroke down the glitter to get any additional pieces not glued down.

Step 9

Add a piece of tape above the glitter line. Do the same to the bottom. Get a plastic cup and gloves.

Step 10

Use the epoxy and measure equal parts of solution A and B into measuring cups. If it's a small mug, you only need about 15 ml each. Larger ones need 20 ml.

Step 11

Pour them both in a cup and scrape down the sides using a wooden stick.

Step 12

Stir for three minutes and pop all bubbles.

Step 13

Your gloves should be on but, if not, put them on now. Add the glitter to the epoxy and stir.

Step 14

Add the mixture to the tumbler and turn it on while you're doing this. Having a roller or something to turn it on will help and make sure it's in the air, so nothing is touching it.

Step 15

When the chemicals aren't coming as fast, you can slow down the speed it turns around.

Step 16

Take the tape off after forty-five minutes.

Step 17

Spin the tumbler for five hours, and it should be dry. If not, leave it on a foam roller overnight.

Step 18

Sand the tumbler gently with wet sandpaper.

Step 19

When it's all smooth from sanding, clean it with rubbing alcohol. Then open Cricut Design Space and cut out your glitter vinyl.

Step 20

Weed the design. Attach a firm grip transfer tape and transfer the decal to the drum.

This is a very complicated project that takes a lot of time, and you need to be sure that children are not near these items, since it would be fatal to them if they ingest them. A further thing to keep in mind is to spin to make sure it's dry. By adopting these directions, you're expected to have a perfect glitter tumbler that you can take anywhere and sport a trendy look. This is a brilliant idea for business owners as well, since customized tumblers are a hot product right now, and everybody loves them.

Conclusion

In this book, we've given you the resources you need to be a better craftsman, and we've also given you useful tips about how to save money with your materials and make sure you've been able to use them for as long as possible. Primarily, the cricut machines weren't thought to be that amazing until people eventually began buying them, and then they found that these machines had so much merit that it was truly useful and worth the effort and the cost.

The best part of this book is that we're giving you true meaning and real understanding of these devices and making you grasp why crafting is so much easier with them. It protects you from hand-cutting and exhaustion, and also fatigue, and the Maker is able to work half as quickly as most. Imagine what you're going to do and how much time you're saving at the speed of this machine! In comparison, three hundred products can be cut where just one hundred can be made by others. We describe the advantages of having this ultimate machine at your hands and how it will actually help your craftsmanship. If you use the strategies we've described in this book, you'll be better off learning to use this machine for the first time. It's not a complex machine, but the knowledge can be daunting at first.

Tools are a huge part of this, too, and we're going to outline how you can find the tools you need for cheaper and how you can't get bad materials that won't work, and how to stop defective tools. The easiest way to get these tools is to get them for the company to make sure that you're getting consistency as well as being able to reap the benefits of fantastic deals and rewards that are unique to the company itself.

We also send you wonderful detail on which machine is cutting what material and what machine is cutting what material. You don't want to buy a gadget that assumes it's going to cut content or a certain function only to find that it doesn't. That's why we got the conjecture out of the way for you. Now that you have a list of which machines can use which products, that can also help you see which machine is going to be the right choice for you and your needs. They're all different and they have various crafting needs. Someone will only need an Explore One just because of that. If this is you, you're going to get the machine you like for you. If you know that you're not going to need your computer as much as you don't need the costliest one possible. You'll just need one if you're going to use this computer every day.

The Cricut machines have four distinct machines and 2 distinct series, as we describe in length as well as the variations and similarities between them. Knowing the nuances between them is going to be equipped to make the most intelligent decision you want. It can help with your budgetary requirements as well, so only you know what you can invest and what you can't. With over one hundred and twenty different tips on how to ensure sure your machine is working correctly, clean tips, supply tips, and even font tips, we've made sure you get the best out of your machine and make sure you're becoming a Cricut expert. We'll also offer you awesome crafts that you'll be capable of making, and you'll be able to make the most of this by beginning with simple crafts before going on to more complex projects as well. The projects we mentioned at the end of the book range from basic to a little more complex, so you can see what we think when we talk about what these devices can do and what they can't do. Note that the Builder is the best of the four and will be able to manage whatever project you like with simplicity and elegance at the same time.

With this book, you're going to be able to comprehend your crafting at a better level with a machine that's built for ease, strength, and you're going to make your dreams come true.

.

CPSIA information can be obtained
at www.ICGtesting.com
Printed in the USA
BVHW060910250321
603396BV00008B/588